Rachmaninoff Masterpieces
for Solo Piano
17 Works

SERGE RACHMANINOFF

DOVER PUBLICATIONS, INC.
Mineola, New York

Bibliographical Note

This Dover edition, first published in 2003, is a new compilation of piano
works originally published separately in authoritative early editions.

International Standard Book Number: 0-486-43122-3

Manufactured in the United States of America
Dover Publications, Inc., 31 East 2nd Street, Mineola, N.Y. 11501

CONTENTS

Prelude in C-sharp Minor

No. 2 of *Morceaux de fantaisie*, Op. 3

Polichinelle

No. 4 of *Morceaux de fantaisie*, Op. 3

Barcarolle

No. 3 of *Morceaux de salon*, Op. 10

Humoresque

No. 5 of *Morceaux de salon*, Op. 10

Moment Musicaux

No. 3 of *Moments Musicaux*, Op. 16

Moment Musicaux
No. 4 of *Moments Musicaux*, Op. 16

Moment Musicaux

No. 5 of *Moments Musicaux*, Op. 16

Prelude in F-sharp Minor

No. 1 of *Ten Preludes*, Op. 23

Prelude in D Major

No. 4 of *Ten Preludes*, Op. 23

Prelude in G Minor

No. 5 of *Ten Preludes*, Op. 23

Un poco meno mosso

Prelude in E-flat Major

No. 6 of *Ten Preludes*, Op. 23

Prelude in B-flat Minor

No. 2 of *Thirteen Preludes*, Op. 32

Prelude in B Minor

No. 10 of *Thirteen Preludes*, Op. 32

Prelude in G-sharp Minor
No. 12 of *Thirteen Preludes*, Op. 32

Etude-tableaux in C Major

No. 2 of *Etudes-tableaux*, Op. 33

Etude-tableaux in G Minor

No. 7 of *Etudes-tableaux*, Op. 33

Etude-tableaux in E-flat Minor

No. 5 of *Etudes-tableaux*, Op. 39